Handing Out Apples in Eden

POETRY

MALISA GARLIEB

Handing Out Apples in Eden

~ POETRY ~

MALISA GARLIEB

Published by
WIND-RIDGE BOOKS of vermont
Shelburne, Vermont 05482

Handing Out Apples in Eden
Copyright 2014 by Malisa Garlieb

All rights reserved. No part of this book may be used or reproduced in any manner whatsoever without written permission except in the case of brief quotations embodied in critical articles and reviews.

Cover design by Laurie Thomas
Back cover photo of author by Tanna Pflaster

ISBN: 978-1-935922-57-5
Library of Congress Control Number: 2014947201

Published by WindRidge Books of VT
PO Box 636
Shelburne, Vermont 05482

Printed in the United States of America

Contents

I. FRONT GARDEN

A stutterer introduces herself 3
The red house, Cedar Circle 5
Birkenwald, 1903 7
Heard 9
Handing Out Apples in Eden 10
Still Life in Oil by Margarite DeMay 11
What is Offered 12
Blueberry Season 13
Odds 14
Sure or Unknown Shore 15
Breakfast Below the Portrait of Lila O. Vanderbilt 16
This New Night 17
Handled 19
After High Water, I Notice 20
Bound 21
Dearest Scot, ... 22
Maudlin Catalog 23
Eastern Gray 25

II. KINDER

Minus Two Times, Four 29
At Two Months 31
First Lesson: that the teacher does not see 32
Mine 34
Plunge 35
Correspondence 36
Tales 37
Let the next thing be a sign 38
For Winston, and other seven-year-old black boys 39
Consequential Fruit 40
Plausible Yarn 41
Cocoon Hardening and Softening 42
Charges 43

v

Long Division 44
Heart—Indigo 46
The Pair 48
Hansel (Gone) 49
Nursery 51

III. BACK GARDEN

Recurring Down-slurred Trill 59
They are not all benevolent 60
At Fourteen 61
Two Crowns 62
Whittle Trance 64
Three Deceits 65
He/She 67
The Inherent Thing 68
Today and Maybe Tomorrow 70
In Art School My Lover Made Two Self-Portraits 72
Katie 74
Hate Her, Edge of Something 76
The Dropped 77
Letter from Home, a place you've never been 78
Keepers 79
Cut & Paste Pastiche 81

Acknowledgements

Grateful thanks to the publications in which the following poems first appeared or are forthcoming:

Painted Bride Quarterly: "Heart—Indigo"

Off the Coast: "Charges," "At Fourteen," and "Breakfast Below the Portrait of Lila O. Vanderbilt"

Compass Rose: "Correspondence"

So to Speak: a feminist journal of language and art: "A stutterer introduces herself" and "Recurring Down-slurred Trill"

Ship of Fools: "Minus Two Times, Four"

Mad Poets Review: "Cocoon Hardening and Softening"

The Salon: "They are not all benevolent"

Sugared Water: "The Pair" and "Blueberry Season"

Lines + Stars: "After High Water, I Notice"

Please Do Not Remove: A Collection Celebrating Vermont Literature and Libraries: "In Art School My Lover Made Two Self-Portraits"

Chautauqua: "The Inherent Thing"

Acknowledgements

I extend gratitude to the many teachers in my life, both inside school walls and without. To Daniel Lusk and The Writers' Barn poets for encouraging these poems to their best expression. To Abigail Diehl-Noble, Kristin Agudelo, Peter Snow, Monica Smith, Gary Margolis, and Paul Matthews who read and helped me shape a manuscript. To Tamra Higgins and Mary Jane Dickerson at Sundog Poetry Center for their willingness to support a newcomer. To Lin Stone, an editor who embodies both kindness and discernment. To Jesse Lee Kercheval, an early influence. For Sueanne Campbell, who knew where the keys were kept. For my students and dear colleagues at LCWS, who keep the balls rolling and the angels busy. For Keenan, my love. For D. and S., with whom I've studied hardest. For J., my celebrant. And especially to my parents, Gary and Pam Garlieb, who indulged my bookish disposition. Thank you.

I. FRONT GARDEN

A stutterer introduces herself

or not, if the syllables come without sound
and the mouth pantomimes
the onset M in white gloves.

She begins with her lips open
so the penned up can slip out
to grass before morning's milking.
Let it always be a county fair in May.
Let moored breath beckon a wheedling wind
before the thunder of big-top speech.
Everyone will look up, necks exposed,
and wait
as the clouds roll in.

So the fluency's flexible,
may a maundering farm hand amble
the meandering mile, and consonants
become malleable when struck
or stuck by the jaw.

But if blocked again again again,
the repetitions of Ma- Ma- Ma-
might call to mind the bleat
of judged goats in the grandstand and
you will feel ashamed
of your adolescent associations.
A trick trap door's underfoot
for moments like this.

Or, if you're kinder sort, maybe instead
you'll hear the infant summoning
Mother (the first sensible uttering)
and notice she's pretty
though her message is mazy.

And if the confusion continues
in this casual meeting of strangers,
I suggest you generously
let her build momentum or cancel
the conversation completely.
Some carousels are silent.
She's looking away.

Letting beginning be easy as ice cream—
licking maple creamees
melty at noon under the oak,
make light contact with your eyes
and her tongue will make light contact
in her mouth. And her larynx will release
the mechanical latch holding back
the tin tine that plays
the music of mute clowns.
The melody holds most of the meaning anyway
and red lipstick smears all the M's.

The red house, Cedar Circle

There are losses
her heart will not trace
whilst the red fox from the lilies
spies on her dream, wife hanging
white sheets
in slatted backyard sun.

A myth begins each day
when spouse
leaves for work, the toddler
builds a topple tower
just to knock it down,
and breakfast dishes sit
rim with flies.

She knows, she needs
to weed
the slugged beds—
bugs in lunch's lettuce
and baby listlessly digging
his parents' slogged soil.

The privations are small.
Stereo's swollen music
turned down, the right
upturned card, a call
from the wrong man

and a love letter through
the slit in her little
sweet life.
No one checks
the mail
but her.

None of this is real
of course
none of it
can be spoken.
She writes back

of honeyed beets
in chocolate bundts,
a trampled border
and how the bittersweet's
pinched the crabapple.
The stamp is gummed
turn turtle
on purpose.

Intending good
to sauce the rhubarb
and cut the amuck
dog rose loose, instead
she pages poetry

in the afternoon chaise
and dinner
will be quick pasta
tailed by
swift bedtime.

Watched,
she takes no wine
to numb her
arch art.
The sleep will be wide
and enough.

Birkenwald, 1903

Klimt paints birch trees
because he once saw
how she opened her blouse
revealing one scar at a time.
The wind braided her skinny
parts and left lissom limbs
trembling, breathy
to neighboring beech.

His mother, he remembers
disrobed in front of the children
without thought. They'd come
from her and dressing
was the only portraiture available.
He leaves the easel now to touch
the stripping bark like he
cannot his mother. His palm
an earnest child soothed,
faint scent of mint.
Lake Attersee can only mean light,
sommerfrische and Emilie—
he adds the blue woodflower,
color of her favored chemise,
to the stippled foreground.

He tries not to think of his father
but the engraver's gold
is leafing from every tree.
Pinnate, ovate, his fall
must be gathered, how sun fingers
the darkness to patterns, pigment
moss of inner woods. How clouds
on the Alps have not rained
on this burning. How one
stand of trees connects to another
and a forest was once all of Europe.
Before kings commissioned cutters,
academia's coffeehouse critics.

Between every daubed tree
is a woman, a guilt, a failure, a ghost,
a wood goblin artist
in only a light blue robe.
Art is a line around your
thoughts. There is nothing
special about me.

Heard

On autumn's first cold evening
I find my hat in parka's sleeve,
and cattle crowd the electric fence
as I approach with too few bruised apples
and unsettled belonging.
All black mass in the dim,
I hardly see their eyes' glint.
A few lows break from dense breathing.
Now among, some fence in me is suddenly slipped
and I join, out loud: *that ribbon of highway
I saw above me that endless skyway—*
Calves freeze first as if remembering. As if
saddle songs reside in one of four stomachs.
A kindergarten teacher once told me
he wooed his inner Simpleton each day,
and as this may be the only song
these beasts will ever hear, I lilt longer,
wanting them to know sweetness before stun.
They all then, these sixty or so brick beef Angus,
advance hooves to my *mezzo forte*.
Suddenly conscious and afraid of stampede,
I turn homeward, humming to placate.
One bull follows the line
to enclosure's edge. I receive his seeing.
Long bovine pleasures of pasture and herd,
hours arriving and arriving
with jaw of yellow birdsfoot.

Handing Out Apples in Eden

She wore red silk to her own wedding—
a wedding her mother would not attend
because the other bride wore blue.
And just to put the cherry on top
red lipstick and toenails, too.
Right red sun chased left blue moon.

Red for luck, red for exclamation,
declaration
and because brash brass bells
cannot be ignored.
There was no church to go to
all the curtains were drawn

but the hearth
hot hot flamed
and when her wife
walked, the long hem of her skirt
wiped up last night's rain.

Still Life in Oil by Margarite DeMay

—my grandmother,
hanging near her kitchen clock

A bruise is acceptable in a pear
as they are peasant stock—

pears' shoulders reveal
the hard mold of muscles
that have carried heavy
sacks of grain

squalling babies have hung
off their hefting hips.

After day's labor
they sit together
at the table.

They cock their heads and nod
consenting
to one another.

What is Offered

I.

There is a rose bush
growing liberally
shadowing savory herbs by spans

    in the thick
untried afternoon,

but it bears   only
one June bloom.

Hardly worth the pruning shears,
    but I

have taken again.

II.

Winter's slow sedation
then summoning,

    an assemblage of light
amending green leaf

to bud to petal
    to petal,
the quiet revolution

the answer
of why
    I take.

III.

A denial of thorn.

Blueberry Season

Six or seven fall simply into my palm,
a few still stemmed but purpling
under the high summer sun.
The technique of thumb rolling
across fingers, fingers then parting to receive
fruit reminds me how you touched
my nipples. The tight twist,
one chord of the exquisite circle
measured and the rest of me longer
on the bed.

If I get enough to cook and sugar
the jam can shine
on the crusts of winter, when light
and memory are shorter and more needed.
Last January our touch couldn't
catch though my body cheated it
and ripened by routine.
I kept checking the pantry of our marriage.
Had enough been put away, is there enough to last?
Twelve lids sealed to glass, all the rims twisted tight.

Odds

a full moon
and grandmothers sit
at Oneida nickel slots

a full moon
and mothers wait in hallways
for graduates to return

a full coin moon
and I rock on a lit porch
silently expecting you

Sure or Unknown Shore

for S—

In dirtier times you'd be taken
in fits and cast out,
fish flapping in electric water.
But medication has cleaned you
kind man. You unknowingly
sleep with angels. Only
the occasional seizure
ripples you down, lightning rod
with a shock of blond.

During confusion and exhaustion the body must be noticed.
Metallic blood on lips and the taste of tongue.

So you sculpt the earth,
pound and solder its ores
tear up the tangly roots.
The sizzle and flash
is grounded again and again.

Doctors say you're lucky.
With tight talons upon scalp
your brain waves are watched
by a flock of electrodes.
Surgical saws can open
your skull like an oyster
and extract the disease
with delicate forks and dainty knives.

Your eyes can swim in fresh lakes
unblinking and dark.
Lured / cured by the dazzle of light on water.

Breakfast Below the Portrait of Lila O. Vanderbilt

Shelburne Farms, Vermont

The peonies past the terrace have a look
of catastrophe about them
what with the rain and the need
for abundance to fall
into spectacular ruin.

Lila is tall in paint
but that may be the art of posture.
Wearing burgundy ribbons
and a mint shawl, despite her coloring
she aches in the absence of cobalt.
Perhaps she didn't know blue.

With peony's pigment on her cheeks
her wrists are not thin but gloved.
Stomach pouchy, chin small
yet her lids are heavy and her breasts in lace.
I stare at her unfittingly.

The server is disquieted
—the abandoned omelette
and cooling coffee with cream—
but the inn's departed heiress
with a gardener's eye for what's gone by
tilts her head down regarding
all my stems leaning, petals on the grass.

This New Night

As he hands her plums she thinks/he is the kind of man who'd kiss her on the lips in friendship/to whom she'd try to turn a cheek in time.
                                        -Maura Dooley

in old flannels you sit
with me on the porch, imperfect
gibbous moon rolling in a peacock sky

raffish boys down the block curse
and run without regard
and my sister's playing ragtime
at the piano inside—
              where are the mothers?

with willfulness salty like the tide
I press my fingernails into your palm
       But you

your lips the dusk of tea
a drop of honey at the neck

              But you

the night is breathing
there is water in the wind

earlier I sat alone beside the plum tree
burdened with blossoms and alive
with bees, big bumbles
and small hummers

      now I am alive with you
and Cassiopeia circling

I want to tell you how yesterday

     the sun's jazz reflected
off the moon's ash
          and never bent but
    highlighted
  your curls—But you

But you
    blushed and grinned
and the light   romped

my stories,
all prior plots and lines learned
are forgotten for instinct
and again the willfulness
      without words

     and again I press
    my nails into your palm

you accept
humming a measure
and go inside
for more tea and blankets

Handled

One neighbor keeps horses
another two sheep.
Tidy fences

of wire and worn circles
and I am happy
to consider

what the lion in my heart
loosed
would make of such docility.

After High Water, I Notice

the driftwood's been cleared
either taken back by the waves or
maintenance

men in green shirts and brown forearms
backs bent in the gesture of service
to the land, the mowed grass, the pruned
scope and view

it seems long that we
gathered together the worn
bleached wood, the white of sky
and blond of my (tossed heart)

Bound

A month before I left her
three months before our tenth wedding anniversary
I collaged the staircase wall
with photos from our life.
I saw it in a home magazine.

Each graytone fact—
our son's second birthday party
a tossed picnic at Shelburne Beach
the mix of strung and slack smiles—
pasted up as proof that I chose it.

When the house sold
I took them down in one abrupt afternoon.
The tea party tore in two, the Christmas angel
floated down unfixed.
I had offered prayers not to fall down this flight.
And the spined architecture of stairs
was now slipped discs all.

I did save one light print
of myself looking off
into light. Don't believe it.
I have uncrissed all ties
and then folded in my top corners.
The bone creaser runs new edges flat
and twine dangles loose desiring knot.

Dearest Scot,

He looked just like you.
Twitchy hands
typing the end table
and his shoulders caving
into complacent slouch.

It's funny because you're a twin,
but it wasn't Dale either
and I'm seeing the whit of shadows.
I live in Vermont now.

His goatee was trimmer, though
I could feel it grizzle
on my hermitic winter skin
from across the waiting room.

I waited a long, long time.

And you eventually did get out of the bed.
What did you tell your wife, anyway?

But don't worry.
The man I saw wasn't you.
The man I saw in you wasn't you.
Go on back to sleep.

You can say you never loved me
and this poem will never get published.

Maudlin Catalog

That night beside the bank's concrete fountain,
lights revising the water from vermillion to green.
How we said some rules don't matter much.

That night it rained after decaf and pots de crème
and we stripped our wet layers in your car,
listening to the Avett Brothers so we didn't need our mouths.

That night we went for pizza, compared high school grades
and let the waitress think it was a date. How we pretended
we were teenagers, doing what neither of us did as teenagers.

That night we danced in my kitchen (wives asleep)
to loose Québécois jazz. A declared non-dancer
finally willing to rock-step, twirl, and pull me in.

That night we got drunk off maple vodka your brother made
and you closed the shades so your neighbors wouldn't see
us standing close, touching lightly often.

That night my dad had just gotten home from bartending
and I entered ruddy, averting speech, and stood at the medicine cabinet
touching the raw skin where you had been.

That night we slowly walked Memorial Dr. to Maier Park,
stopping under willows and glittery steel moons at Discovery World.
You gave me earrings and took off your sandals.

That night after boating and splashing each other silly,
when we entwined fingers and Wendell Berry's metaphors
into our own. The narrow doorway between us open.

That night you sat behind me on Bradford Beach,
your forehead between my shoulder blades,
like two puzzle pieces missing from our marriages.

That night we dressed up, went to a gallery show
and ate fancy food on the patio. Both of us in linen,
in love, watching August lightning in a blaze pink sky.

That night you told me if only you'd met me first,
that we could've been happy, but that you wanted
your life, if not your wife, and day would not come.

Eastern Gray

for D—

In those last loitering days we three lived together,
you were outside painting the house for sale, our son
snacking at the long table. You entered comic and quiet
to say baby squirrels were playing by the swing set. Come see.
No hesitation, our son walked directly and crouched, cooing to them.
Wild creatures on large paws scuttered up his arm and shoulder.
We, afraid of rabies and maybe each other, told him to be careful,
but he grabbed their middles like kittens and smiled. You took
a picture on your phone. This last charm of unbroken us.

II. KINDER

Minus Two Times, Four

conception—

I only need one
perhaps a plum
that does not die within

                      o little seed
             sex
     of the tree
withhold in this body
that does
and does not want
one more foreign object

batten down
and I will make love
until you explode into twins / 2 sets

duplicates so the originals will not be lost

they'll fall out of me
my brood of boys
one for each man I've
lost or will lose / when luck runs out
(and 2 extra just in case)

one for the boy running track
who falls down flat
a heart attack
at age 19

one for the patient
tender man
whose brain's to be carved
with trembling hand—
ending epilepsy

should such things be rhymed?

and when I've raised them kind
four sons for the directions
they'll come saying sing-song
look what we've found

and I'll smile because I got what I wanted
you've been vigilant, I'm good at hiding

my men

At Two Months

*It's a successful day when, at the end of it,
you're both still alive.*
–lactation consultant

when my pool was cut open
they pulled a pink mammal
insisting
and predictable in his need

fleshy fists pound my breastbone
as he guzzles blue milk
that drips from me at four a.m.

this is the only rhythm—
each day dropping sleep
and feedings on demand
in a grab bag of hours spent

I used to collect time
selfishly like pearls—
what to do today, tomorrow
but now the necklace
is dangled before him
to swat and take
my leisure

I've given up counting
ounces gained, little piggies,
the hours before
spouse returns home guilty

only his smiles now—
each chiming high in tinny tones
breaking, as though my swaddle alone
could sustain him, my held breath

First Lesson: that the teacher does not see

Dirty dolls declined in the house corner
and a pennant alphabet swagged above
the low boat tables and carpet islands.

Chipped chinaware, worn wooden cradles
and the elusive feeling of at-home-anywhere
belonged to girls with beaded barrettes and ballet flats.

Cat-a-corner and partitioned with peg board
the block nook assailed with its big
stump and hammers, the danger of nails and boys.

During playtime, I preferred the paper station
where one worked solitary.
A hole punch was a tool I could handle, my goodness

having two handles and fitting in one hand.
Some days I made piles of confetti for Mr. Nobody's birthday party.
Sometimes one lone star smiled back from the black table.

Teacher's desk in the corner blocked access
to the craft closet, chamber of treasures, but here
was the hoard set out by a literate angel.

Arranged freshly each day, were selections
from the pillars of colored cardstock, cartons of pom-poms,
googly eyes, and jars of gold glitter.

I knew to cut on solid lines only.
I knew how to drizzle glue without puddles.
Mrs. Morey liked me. I had memorized

Chicken Soup with Rice and had recited it to her
before the bell, mostly without stuttering.
To touch her skirt was to be safe in adult dominion.

Maybe because a hole is finite and final.
Maybe because a punch makes room for a brad
jointing a puppet's elbow, allowing a friendly wave.

Maybe because isolation makes one petite hole at a time
I took the paper punch. I slid it down my tights,
eggshell and cable-knit under a velveteen jumper.

All day it sat in the cotton crotch, the hot pocket
created by my long legs. During Red Rover it slipped
to my thigh and I discreetly shimmied it back up.

No one knew it was there during story time
sitting criss-cross-applesauce. No one knew who was there
next to Tony, cutting out wordless blue clouds.

And only when home, in the privacy of the bathroom
did I pull down my tights and regard the gadget
that provided the quiet glee of a private punch back.

Mine

the bucket is half full of water
and leaves and sticks float
as boat or food for the captured

He's my magic beetle
my son pronounces with a hard tacking T
      not the flat deh of my Midwestern
        farmer's disdain for crop eaters

his beetle is an emerald and cocoa cabochon
a wonder
a swimmer
a climber
a pet
      to be guarded and pushed around
       and made to stay put where placed

his affection for this insect grows
with the day's heat
but the bug wearies / I worry what I'll do
when it dies

but I don't intervene—
this life belongs to the unknowing boy now
and he never sees the end

the beetle loses its shine and falls
into tangled grass, ignored at last
and I've done this
to him—beetle and boy

Plunge

for Zeke and Finn

*We are newborn
which means we're mostly dead*
one boy announces to the other.

Unchallenged, agreement implicit
they continue playing baby polar bears
in a dining chair igloo.
After catching *(I hardly know how to/
just pretend)* plastic fish
they gut and gorge breakfast, ignore
the boy-rule of tough, and cuddle up
until mama bear returns.

Then they flip the coin
and throw themselves
off a couch, off the edge into extinction
into the lake blue carpet.
Losing the instinct of swim
the cubs drown in giggled delirium.
They enact the gasping,
gulping, rolling, grasping
do it like this spectacle
of transition into
new elements.
They know more about death, at seven
than their parents imagine.

In utero of the grown-up world,
headlong to light and birth,
two boys break water.

Correspondence

the sun is low in the window
and my four-year-old son
enters the bedroom
he knows what I've been doing
paper, pen, words slowly coming

he holds out his supplies
blue construction paper and a yellow pencil
I'm going to write poetry too
and he does

ticks, dashes, array and ancient meaning
before the knowing of alphabet
his efforts are all straight lines and they glow on
the dark paper nightfall

Mama what does it say?
but I don't know
what lies within him
and I falter

he reconsiders, studying the effect of formula
and states his two great purposes
Love
Keenan

Tales

He asks again
for the story of three bears
and the girl, and encounters in the woods.
I read it once and now he's pestering.

I want to say I don't remember
that once upon a time has passed—

it's the damn satisfaction, the just-rightness
of those chairs and beds and pies
that rubs and I go on stirring
plain porridge with a wooden spoon.

I want instead to tell how living
with the want
has its own sweet way,
but my son's already learned to read me
and knows that one.

let the next thing be a sign

shake of frog or shriek
of spinning girl
mean the same for second grade:
spring

when teachers laugh
the tire swing is warm sway
and Rosie wants to play chase again

popping dandelions
their feet get tangled in *teddy bear, teddy bear*
wheeling ropes and snake holes

hardened hearts break into bleeding blossoms
and pockets are stuffed
with lilacs that soothe
more than mothers can anymore

forced inside they chew on wide syllables
in Brer Rabbit tales
in leaves of leveled readers
while picking the monkey bar blisters
on rubbed-raw palms

For Winston, and other seven-year-old black boys

who struggle with capitalization and spaces
between words
        that
              dribble
                    on dotted lines

I decide
he must become
a griot
else no one will hear
the stories of seven—
            cats under the porch
            and grandma in a wheelchair

write it down
you're important / no recess
until you write it
            down

later I pray (do lord
remember me) that he
will publish in scholarly journals
how teacher
                messed
        with the black boys

Consequential Fruit

The pear's for later,
heavy and ripe-resting
beneath brindled skin.

Now needs a swifter jaw
a crisper bite than the mash
of November.

Apples are falling
out of my control.
I pick a few each day.

The tree holds my son's swing
as he climbs higher.

For him, at six, there's only one world
one branch of belong.
Though one day he'll glimpse Eve,

her dazzle obscuring the bark's foothold
the next bough down. He'll divide
himself from divinity

a boy on a tree / no longer in.

How the apple
of childhood's read rightly,
grace arriving through will or sudden time—

bark grating skin, smarting rose sores.
Reminders amid ripening.

Plausible Yarn

Tucking my boy under knit coverlet,
I kiss his peppermint breath
when he asks, already swimming
in it, *What is sleep made of?*

I'm inclined to skein out another
made-up tale on *The Land of Sleep*
where angels accompany dreamers
like acrobats between images, but

he's not so easily answered anymore.
Having seen how one dropped stitch
unravels winter's sweater,
how loved ones drop out of contact,
that not all arguments end
with apologies.

I hand him his first bear, buying time
but his drooped eyes blank and then fix—

Black, he says, meaning nothing.

Devastated, I acknowledge
with a compact nod. Pause,
become mother adding, *but behind
the blackness are dreams,
and behind the dreams…*

and he's spun again, flung
on the drop-spindle of sleep.

Cocoon Hardening and Softening

We're walking home from Woolworth's
when the man winks at me
and mom says flatly
she's fourteen.

Entering eighth grade at six feet
my body cannot hide me.
So I slouch, wear drab
and stop talking altogether.
The sullen silence wears my neck
like nubby silk
torn from a sari and knotted.
My stutter—dear foe—
gave too much away.

Now stifled syllables calcify
as little stones in my stomach.
Each holding a word
that jumbles as I jump
into a poem
that reveals me once again.

Charges

for eighth graders studying science

I wish to name all the boys
after flowers
for their fists unfurl
and drink the rain
Mud lines their pockets and they speak
languages of touch and impetus:
jostle, push, lean, reach

The bloodroot, trillium, and bluet are ephemeral
brief as the boyhoods that roll into sweaty games
and spiked lemonade at dusk
(then there are the girls waiting for consideration)

I wish to name these girls
for their mica glint in granite, their patience
the veins of metal ore that liquefy under heat
soldering one to another,
for the silica that both obscures
and admits light passage (the list grows
long as they have words that name
the phenomena of density)

Their rutile hearts and heavy hips tip
the balance of the stars
and weigh the sky

Earth and cloud together
with lightning racing between the poles
make a battery
Voltage unavoidable, daring and desired
they find each other

Long Division

$$
\begin{array}{r}
38\ \text{r.}1 \\
3\overline{\smash{)}115} \\
-9 \\
\hline
25 \\
-24 \\
\hline
1
\end{array}
$$

Call it a house—
a divisor always knocking at the front door.
Begin: how many 3's in 11?
Three make a family, pairs of lost mittens
by naughty kittens, baskets
on the mudroom floor.

Take the 9 months of 2 ribs kicked
from the inside. Mother's heart
propelled by the bruiser. Force
of gate. Of gale.

Bring down the 5 years a family
before she left to live
in a one-bedroom basement,
life's tedium
written out,
       indented
              and
                     descending.
What's left
and how many 3's in a last shiny quarter?
That summer, 8 times they counted-out
saved change.

Low back out, foundation slipped,
she could barely walk the block
for a root beer treat.
Baby carried the purse.

The quotient 38, her age, appears after
subtracting 24 months of separation,
but a remainder of 1
before Solomon—
    child who cannot / be split,
but somehow must be shared.

These should be friendlier numbers
and they shall have no pie.

Heart—Indigo

They're a twenty-eight volume set
sixth grade reading level, already fifteen years old.

The last box to be moved
I take them out to the station wagon
four at a time, filling the passenger's seat.
I think of them as a person.
Knowledge as gathered and edited
humanity passed along in the code of words,
the medium of trees.

A friend asks why I'm saving relics
and I say that we are deceiving ourselves
in ciphers these days—
weightless zeroes, ones, and lit zipped files.
Archivism is being lost to digits that mean letters
that mean someone had an idea once
upon a long time past.
But they are really for my son.

Someday when he can read I think he might
pick up the *heart—indigo* volume,
page through it and learn something
of the way both seep and bleed.
And hearing how I carried these into our new apartment
after the divorce, up the stairs
and saved them for his tenth birthday
he'll understand what he's felt but couldn't name.
Encyclopedias are good for naming.

He'll lay the heaviness on his lap and fathom the effort
of accumulation, the weight of memory, the separateness
of himself, of his parents
in the lost treasure of ink on the canvas of trees.

The Pair

Hallelujah for sun in February so we walk
the afternoon and I hold his wrist
so his mitten won't fall off—
its mate left to the mismatch bin.
His little feet lift the boots Vermont requires,
thick-soled waterproof and vermillion.
Flame boots that will not get left
behind somewhere.

His father, or rather the man I want
to father him, lives
with a wife a thousand miles west.
He may choose us someday. Maybe not.
My son isn't speaking, which is unusual,
and I think he knows I have no answers

anymore and damn it, why can't he walk
without shuffling. Pick up your feet child.
But then I see his over-big boots are
on the wrong feet.

You'd be more comfortable, I say
if you switched your shoes,
but he keeps up the clodding.
And then I know
as a lamb knows cold spring,
how we choose our slow suffering.
And that we could
end it with a swap—boot
or stubborn heart.

Hansel (Gone)

Because he keeps me
like a stone in his pocket,
my son arranges a date
for my birthday—
he's dressed himself up in corduroy
and cajoled my ex into matinee
tickets and cookie money.
He holds my hand in the black
box theater but is gone with the lights
and first jangling gestures of marionettes.
Gone choiceless along a path
of subconscious story and angels
who won't let you roll a cliff's edge.
Now I lay me down to sleep,
I pray the Lord my soul to keep.
Is life really that shining?
I mean, the evidence:
a failing moon, crumbling crusts
and stain of black walnuts.
A lashed branch is false assurance
you're not alone in the woods.
Having read Bettelheim and Bly,
having worn more costumes
than capes in my years,
I stay determinedly detached
from the staged Black Forest.
I refuse to enter again the longing for those
who do not want me, my cage
somehow cold next to the oven.

I've been the hooked witch
living off sweetarts
and fat-fingered children,
walked the weird parallels
with their allure of truth and core.
And when the hour's up
and he's ventured far into archetype,
returning upon a swan's back,
his eyes shine with the intact belief
in a father who hugs us all home.
We speak little of the show
and I eat both our cookies.

Nursery

1.
Rhyme

I'm a woman who loves a woman,
I'm a woman in love with a man.
I've planted my heart, it may grow in a knot
from doing the best that it can.

2.
And the cock crowed even after

her tendrils ran
down a mountain
and tongue, a wild violet
suckled the morning star
dimming at dusk

the girth of her
flesh and wonder
exhaust the thought
of carrying on
to the cleared forest where
polite women make wooden
bells with wooden clappers

a witch cannot
make conversation
as she raises her heavy arm
to ring the sun gong
parting the thighs of the blue-
willow sky

3.
Solstice

And the grass is wet as I tend herbs—
the cilantro a bird
that chirps a light-hearted freeing
of the sun in love and flaming.
Tonight the light gambols until nine
and the owl, ruler of order, sleeps.
Without the yellowed eyes scanning
what will get away
what desire will be met
what shadow—self will find a bed?
The petite warbling
and churning of swallows
round the myth of you entering me
without ink on the deed or the third key.
Defiantly, I forsake the hour when gods
glitter pure and nonchalant.
I wait for the dark.

4.
Catch of Passion

the bear prince sleeps in cattails
brittle stalks as broken bed
for the son that shines but fails

between shaming and grasses
I'll lie down naked like twigs

our love is disappointment—
each apple bruised and wormy
and I desire your weight still

I've unmasked all the magic
powers possible or not
and white horses kneel like flames

oblique against the expanse
of hope, my heart as your wish
your wish smelling of cedar
branches in my hair undone

5.
Then a Narrative

When you dream a silver wood
and strike the branch
and your marriage dead

When the birch bows and whimpers
your name meaning now
and the time of bells claps a heart

When a mud cottage and roof
of golden straw bed the stars
and you trade books for brooms

When the basket's full of clove cake
heavy with oblong plums and you
sit at my table meaning it

6.
Primer Vocab.

AP·ple
   fruit of Eve, fruit of childhood:
   Eat all the apples, the all of apples—
   pips of poison, petal flesh, and witch's stars within.

a·BAN·don
  a word nonexistent in some languages,
  in Latin *'to control'*

COUNT
  recitation of number, to be significant
  or of value to someone:
  Begin to count—you'll end up
  short—the Grimmer sides of fountain coins.

7.
Shoemaker takes a turn at hunting

You know the ending
when you're in the middle
and he calls you from his cobbler's bench
out of earshot from his wife

and asks, when did the world
first curve in, and when did I
first see it? Make staylaces answer—
stay the answer he wants.

(He does not know
there is nowhere he has been in you
that has not eyed the edge.)

Say yes, my love, you wholly belong
to her and sylvan shadows.

There is too much earth to love. So saying,

lay his head on stone to sleep
but patient watch the flapping cape—
black flapping wings before dawn brings
the forgetting of mountains in snow.

Slack-jaw to White's tranced tropes—
miners' birds, mouthing mirrors
and suicide on display—

he listens and wants

wants to listen of love he cannot extend
but wants the hushing
to tell him again.

Give in. You have mapped this wood.

In this auspicious time,
she said and said,
the huntsman thought
he spared her heart.

8.
Rhyme

tongue without kiss
speech without sound
heart without mate
rule without crown

home without roof
time without clock
hope without promise
key without lock

lock without door
boat without dock
you left me
in flight without flock

III. BACK GARDEN

Recurring Down-slurred Trill

One nest contained 52 hairpins, 188 nails, 4 tacks, 13 staples, 10 pins, 4 pieces of pencil lead, 11 safety pins, 6 paper clips, 52 wires, 1 buckle, 2 hooks, and 3 garter fasteners.

–Joan Dunning, *Secrets of the Nest*

All the junk of our lives finally
finds a use when we dress ourselves as wrens—
The male builds first nest,
tail cocked and wanting her dismantling.
For days after, both birds join and build till
the breadbox near bursts with twigs of her choosing.
The eggs were laid one by one
in rumpled sheets of spring.
But when you did not return,
we assumed you dead and birdlings
fledged by speckled night. I do not know if wrens
mate for life and may no one tell me, so
I repeat the dream of weave and winding,
a beak to bind, and gathering of bits.

They are not all benevolent

after Rudolf Steiner

I must describe the malevolent ones—
this element already present in man
begetter of parasites
and the trickery that exists in this world

Everywhere there are snares
and down below processes are taking place
filth dispensed, disintegration

Look at the deadly nightshade
kissed in its flower by the sylph

At Fourteen

The doctor places his hand inside me
the place no one's touched
and a crow flies out of my head
The needle comes again
kits and labs and tubing clutter the rolling tables
and my fingers become caterpillars that won't make it
to safety and dark pods

The sheet and my mother's face are white and cornered
and I see it from above
My body smaller and smaller on the bed
distant from me suspended

Then the minute moves backward—
the marionette's released
and falls back into gravity, potential and pain
The tension held in the strings between,
between childhood and maturity
between this here and the next,
angle into fourteen's nascent curves
and become my body's bearing

Two Crowns

O Madonna
      attendant of night
      and keeper of star secrets
      humble me to decency

      swaddle in your cloak
          a fighter in the folds

O Magdalene
      my flesh is white
      all else close in waiting
      —the red egg faultless

      black is the rood of my singing
      each weeping, wooden
      pitches I teach the herons

      ravens resist my lessons
          rightly

O Mistress
      lover of the body
      you took him in your mouth
      loved the tilt and tip of his hip
          and opened the earth for him
      for practice

      how finds
      the one kind king

O Mary
    maker of a man
    teach me to bear it

    the inflamed tendernesses
    the thorns already blooming

Whittle Trance

For the form,
for my bird emerging from maple
my body braces like a vise
and a blade carves blond wood in upward curves
into the grain.

Dense heartwood of your will,
the impenetrable hour against the chisel
is time to repeat the cheeping vowel
of your name. Warp of nest
and weft of this song insistent
come from a dark beak, for a future of eggs.

Wooden boats float, but a fledgling
flies in dreams and wakes wary
of height and risk. Point of creation turn
in patterns of flocking, assured
in currents invisible, the social geometry
and instinct of wayfinding.

I battle the edge with a diamond stone
and the knife is honed—
the mind's skein sharpened, or the lemniscate
between us glinting. Wings desire wind.
So then wind desires wings, I'm sure.

Rubbing the finest grit at the goose's neck
the soft dust gathers dull, but my thumbs
polish unconscious when I think you.

Three Deceits

A. Wyeth's *Night Hauling*

    1 [*night*]

Night's made of wooden slats. Some men have latches.
Thieves put into night and sometimes a man steps into a boat.
Cages are found around sharp or beautiful objects. I mean men.
Boats move precious things into new hands. Let me restate:
The shore doesn't have him. The shoreline does.
In quarter profile, chin and bluff, he's doing no one a favor.
The blind spot is where the action—risk slips through Maine.

A rival steals what's pinned in place, what's left vulnerable.
A lobster is valuable and rivals pin us, live catch.
Where cheat is the action, risk nabs and murmurs treasure.
Some men prepare for the consequences, some not.
Jealousy is a white glow and a trace bullet. It picks locks, too.
Tempura listens to dark water. Night is disobedient.
Water's the blind spot the painter wants to steal.

    2 [*living light*]

Pours of phosphorescence make remote galaxies accessible.
Sea thief, star thief. Worth is a wondrous plankton light. Strange stars.
Softness on edges, luminescence of life, the lambent noctiluca disturbed.
Navy-black dapple-dazzled ripples hook nebulae into tipping.
Less accessible men, less accessible nights. A half-state.
Radiolarian skeletons, millions of them dead, white everything in the wake.
Half enchantment in a dory is a latch. A covert lust breaking.
What should be eerie isn't. This is the milky sea.

3 [capture]

Dark values. Light values. The diagonals.
He's a furtive hunch in waders, sneaking in sleep hours.
His weight and the trap tip the boat's mouth forward. The diagonals.
A back pull to secure the baited swimmers, he lifts and looks left.
A search light can be a fuse of natural phenomena.

The only verticals, his ear and falling water.
The oar is obtuse to escape and parallel to rooked posture,
the black collar, the black bluff, the set jaw.
All other angles acute and dishonest. A jumpy jack.
Imagine the boat is prose and your lover in robber's gloves.
The oar speaks the question the draining water answers. Heaving.
Dishonesty will always look back at the shore, but row away.
Off balance, scuttling of live lobsters in a cage curved like the clawing.
A shoreline brinked with shine slime can give the crook away.

Giving away means latches.
Dawn's near, morning will wave him on.
Keel and slip of stolen, of rope line, of wrist, of wanting, of him, of latches.
Lightening sky, light like lightning in the water, not reflected but in the water.
Notice his thieving, the thieving, the breathing, not breathing, get
the reeling feeling, teeming sea prize gleaming. The diagonals.
Unlatch the hatched, the sometimes latches, the captured luster.
Notice the unnoticed, the man the boat's listing.

He / She

Change: my beloved could only jangle it
in his pocket, afraid of its actual trajectory.
I told him he didn't want my love, he said no.

He couldn't take it. Couldn't take the best of me,
so I administered my worst. Words
meaning nothing in a decade when texting

is the lowest form of language. Icons
and misspellings insulting even when intent is good.
I was mal and badly, went quickly obsolete.

My former wife frauded me thousands
and asserts she should raise the child
a not-my-doctor cut from me. I hemorrhage,

call and call for nurse. They tell me to use
the button. I've looked and tell you there is no button.
Maybe the neighbors will sense something's up.

There was one season I felt my heart,
like one feels the twisted ankle or tweaky back
in the backdrop of a day. Time is dilute now

though a boy is learning to open his hands and track
a ball's arc—the one moment of catch coming.
I tell him he is good. There was a time when I was, too.

The Inherent Thing

*What the eyes perceive in herbs or stones or trees
is not yet a remedy; the eyes see only the dross.*
     - Paracelsus

If I believe in the Doctrine of Signatures,
that curved kidney beans benefit my actual kidney,
the tucking folds on walnuts support neo-cortex knowing,
and avocados, taking nine months from blossom
to ripened fatty fruit, strengthen stretched womb,
then I can see the signs he left, before he left.

Let me describe the ring.

He made me this ring, he said
so I would never again be lost to him.
Night obsidian, bearing no warmth
of its volcanic making, cut oblong and domed
set in silver. No sparkle. All secret
like mute one a.m. walks along Lake Michigan
illicitly holding hands. We were both married then.

The little dipper is stamped in the inner band,
the one fixed star a marker of what will not change.
He put it on my finger, kissed my neck,
and then tossed me to the farthest reaches
where I didn't recognize even one constellation.
I've bought three astrology books, but I still
can't figure out why he never came looking.
What is the anchor of North, the center point of circles
if it is not love?

It's been a year in blankets since—

To believe in the Doctrine of Signatures,
mark how the ever-distending universe
disbands those seven far-flung stars.

Today and Maybe Tomorrow

Upon dawn, dreams
dissipate and I white-knuckle hope
on weak coffee.
The Dalai Lama said western women
will save the world.
Here's what I've got planned for today.

I.
It's impractical, but I want to paint
the southern exposure
rose madder genuine,
the heady blushed hue of dalliance.
Light always eats the darkness
and this fugitive red will fade
to bland tan with time.

> Lightfast, fasten, to hold
> him fast is fiction and
> my dream each night in June.

By July I will know better.
Think of beach towels bleached
on the line.

II.
At noon I'll sit on the floor
and meditate as the blue sky
brightens to the high sun.
The single visible celestial form—
the obvious orb—
is liberal with its light.

I used to stand with stars
but could rarely find the ones
I was looking for. The effort
of directionality and domed degrees
required to find Pleiades upsets
a quiet night. Their unmapped pull
too like the shoulder my cheek once knew.
They gaze at me too softly
and I want to believe them.

This moment only.
Anything broader
and I fall and fall.
I now sleep
ignoring the illusory hilt,

        full tilt
and jilt of night.

In Art School My Lover Made Two Self-Portraits

One was of wire,
a sculpture of air and line.
Crimped deception of matter
with wide internal spaces.

One was a print,
and he pointed out
the trench and boots
blocked in flat black ink.

The third piece
he showed me was a portrait
of his roommate
mild in sleep, unaware.

I've read in Steiner's lectures,
library discard, that as we age,
our feelings, thoughts,
and will in the world

find coherence. Or can.
The alignment's a sign
of maturity,
but all I could think of

was how as a child I put
coins into the collection
at church to fund missions
to inner China.

How ready to patron
a questionable cause,
ignorant of the questions.
My innocent alacrity.

Wanting a more recent example,
I then thought of his work.
And abashed,
I charily closed my purse.

Katie

While her husband
pressed my knee
under a picnic table,
she was in Italy
painting green elephants
with golden nimbi.

We skyped once
and she told me
my long hair made me look
a Magdalene.
She had seen enough
of them. Galleried.
Her husband in the kitchen
cooking me breakfast.
She gave the spare key
years ago,
I shook out her rugs.

After our week,
I put him on a plane
for Florence. She wanted
a second honeymoon.
He wrote me a poem
and saw us
in the masterpieces.
Iconic David,
Venus about to be draped
in red. Nudes.

When I saw the digitals,
wan smiles ate gelato
but mostly
clipped classical gardens,
carved doors,
statuary.
And the elephant
asking how could you
disremember.

Hate Her, Edge of Something

Blue banners everywhere alert tourists
that Shelburne, Vermont turns two hundred-fifty.
The village center boasts boutiques, antiques,
Kevin's Wine & Coffee, and German-made toys.
Incredibly, even an Americana art museum.
Two miles out, on the main road in, Route 7 semis
rankle a Midwesterner's dreams. At least in winter
I can close the windows cutting night's roar, cutting night.
Stressed my wrecked Subaru won't pass inspection,
rent costs half my schoolteacher's income.

Late summer now, and I've come to the co-op
for iced tea and a cool spot to sit. A slim woman
in yoga pants pushes a cart full—count six fillets
salmon on compostable trays, a pineapple, black plums,
ginger kombucha, goat yogurt, local mesclun…
I can't see bottom, though my checking keeps hitting it,
I'll come back on payday for the bulk section.
Their ten varieties of rice pair nicely with the assortment
of organic dried beans. I won't bring my son as he
asks for things and I'm avoiding the words *can't afford.*

I didn't say I used to live on a wooded cul-de-sac
a hop from where my apartment sits on the sidewalk,
buses passing every half-hour. A cute cape with gardens,
built-ins and dishwasher. Divorce takes it all.
Disposed of privacy, I do like to take walks
on gravel farm roads behind the rental. My landlord
owns the cattle farm, shopping center, an electric repair.
I've seen a blue heron twice and a mother with fawns
at the tier of sumacs where I watch sun colors fade.
I'm committed to remaining. What have I ever owned?

The Dropped

How many apples will the wind shake today?
Each bough perhaps unburdened by one or two,
still summer green. The sun is not long here,
but we are blessed in the valley by seven extra days.
Just enough heat to ripen the Cortlands
and Paula Reds. Enough time
to bring baskets and pull the high branches.
Ava will wear a hat and Jack will mostly watch.
There will be enough for winter pies.
And those on the ground—
there is tenderness for those that fall,
a bending in the sour clover.

Letter from Home, a place you've never been

You will know it when you wake rested
and the day is to look forward to—
smile of good neighbors and leaving better
than you found. Everyone plays euchre
in the upstairs-downstairs house and hearts
are always trump. (Minor cheating's overlooked.)
Meals consist of colors: oranges, eggs and greens,
cider and sauce off Johnny Appleseed's broadcast.
You will know the beloved garden
by the scalloped wood lilies at your ankle,
the deep shade under the ash. A bronze eagle's
in the backstory, and at its feet, a shaggy bough
born of a hexal-trunked tree. Under moss, an epitaph:
  When he flew away
    my heart tried to vacate
      and follow, like a kite
        wanting a pitched wind.
It happened to a stranger long ago, but everyone
still thinks it sad. Children play quietly, spreading
their arms over its hollow metal wings or the left bower.
Wishes are unnecessary here as Fate is a fun uncle
with a moustache. He answers the phone politely
and gives directions. Was it you on Tuesday evening?
I wish you were here, but then I forget. Yesterday
was a blue dress and haircut. Time is not much to mark.

Keepers

I'm not supposed to
know this
but there's a lion
in the North wood.

The twin white wolves
streaking green boundaries
with wishes on their tails
know all about him.
Patient red ox
and doves devout
in the stable know.
Even the owl who
keeps trying to gift
me her wings.

Mostly he sleeps
but I have seen
him pacing from
my view on the bough
I might fall from.
My camouflage slipping.

I crave his mane
and imagine carding out
the tangles, burying my face
in matted tawn.

If I asked
I'm sure he would
let me
as these are my trees.
But there is no permission
asked or given. Yet.

Only certainty that
he too is on
our side.

Cut-&-Paste-Pastiche: Matisse's Vence Chapel, France, 1951

What takes place between us is like a shower of flowers—
rose petals that we throw at each other.

> –Henri Matisse in a letter re. Sister Jacques-Marie
> (née Monique Bourgeois), chapel collaborator

M, why did you agree to pose for me?
    I'd never worn a dress with such a low front.
    I got to eat an orange from the painting.

If this is a chapel and you're not religious, what is tenderness?
    The windows are sapphire, emerald and frosted lemon.
    They cast the complement mauve.

M, what is perspective?
    Giving the right impression, you *fleurt*.
    What I got from you.

M, how goes this friendship?
    The mural, Stations of the Cross are few lines to tell
    the whole arc. Less clutter, more impact.

So why did we never—
    I knew you never would. It was enough to paint
    you bare-armed, before vows, wearing my jewelry.

M, what is color?
    A spectrum flung, reckoning white tile.
    The body risen.

No, what is color?
> The world's motif. Archetypes deeper than logic.
> Where I work with a mind close to prayer.

M, why the confessional?
> Door opens blue and closes rose.
> My God, how Jesus suffered!

M, what is God?
> For the courage to see.
> Flowers, these anemones, like candles.

Then what is love?
> A collaboration for beauty. Tabernacle.
> Agglomerate altar of stone like brown bread.

M, what is art?
> A child leaping from the heart of a virgin.
> The image of St. Dominic I draw with my eyes closed.

No, what is love?
> Brilliant vestments and bandage.
> No regrets. AVE.